CPSIA information can be obtained
at www.ICGtesting.com
Printed in the USA
LVHW021632191218
601075LV00030B/2313/P

9 781537 029825